stupid hope

books by jason shinder

Poetry

Stupid Hope
Arrow Breaking Apart
Among Women
Every Room We Ever Slept In

Anthologies

The Poem I Turn To: Actors and Directors Present Poetry That Inspires Them
The Poem That Changed America: "Howl" Fifty Years Later
Birthday Poems: A Celebration
Tales from the Couch: Writers on Therapy
Eternal Light: Grandparent Poems
More Light: Father and Daughter Poems
First Light: Mother and Son Poems
Divided Light: Father and Son Poems
Lights, Camera, Poetry!: American Movie Poems
The Best American Movie Writing (Series Editor)

stupid hope

Poems

Jason Shinder

Graywolf Press

Publication of this volume is made possible in part by a grant provided by the Minnesota State Arts Board, through an appropriation by the Minnesota State Legislature; a grant from the Wells Fargo Foundation Minnesota; and a grant from the National Endowment for the Arts, which believes that a great nation deserves great art. Significant support has also been provided by the Bush Foundation; Target; the McKnight Foundation; and other generous contributions from foundations, corporations, and individuals. To these organizations and individuals we offer our heartfelt thanks.

Stupid Hope includes poems from Jason Shinder's last revised manuscript, and some additional poems found in drafts and journals after the author's death. The texts of the poems are published here intact as the author left them. The author appointed friends and poets Sophie Cabot Black, Lucie Brock-Broido, Tony Hoagland, and Marie Howe as his literary executors, who are responsible for the final organization and editing of this book.

Published by Graywolf Press
250 Third Avenue North, Suite 600
Minneapolis, Minnesota 55401
All rights reserved.

www.graywolfpress.org

Published in the United States of America

ISBN 978-1-55597-533-3

Library of Congress Control Number: 2008941983

Cover design: Kyle G. Hunter

Cover art: Marc Chagall, The Dream, 1939. © 2008 Artists Rights Society (ARS), New York / ADAGP, Paris. The Phillips Collection, Washington, D.C.

Contents

part one

The Pitch of Childhood   3
The Alder Tree   4
First Time   5
My Twentieth Century   6
Saved   7
Middle Age   8
Something Beautiful   9
Pigs   10
The Birthday   13
Fifty   14
How I Am   15
Living   16
Eternity   17
Arrow Breaking Apart   18
Smoke   19
Summer Night   20
Travelers Anonymous   21
Photograph   22

part two

The Good Son   25
The New Year   26
The Story   27
Hospital   28
Finally, It Comes   29
The Change   30
Provincetown   31
Poetry   32
The Return   33
Daughter   34
Jacksonville, Vermont   35
Hope   36

part three

Appointment 39
Afterwards 41
Sickness 42
Bone Marrow Transplant 43
Killing Frost 44
The Knot 45
Reverie 46
Winter 47
Paris, 1980 48
Life After We Know It 49
October 50
Company 51
If You Want to Know 52
Coda 53
The Source 54

part four

The Party 57
Upon Hearing the Experimental Drug Did Not Work 58
Tuttle Crossing, Ohio 59
Fall 60
Looking for Ohio 61
Afterbody 65
Ocean 66
Between 67
At Sunset 68
Alone for the Fifth Day 69
Not Sleeping 70
Untitled 71

Afterword 73

No disease like hope.

     —Hindu Proverb

part one

The Pitch of Childhood

The whipped soul, the whacked and wounded self,

the bleeding bowels, the suffocating shadow,
the post-war flashing star in the broken bottle

of the nation, I had acute something the matter

with me. I was the absence I made of myself as I sat
in a soft chair. I was the lost piece of the moon rocket

that never fell to earth. I was faster than the eagle

on the back of the quarter I tossed into the bay.
I was the letter on the oval desk of the president.

I could not receive. I could not be received.

The Alder Tree

When I think of how my mother shut down—

like the water fountain in the town square when the cold
months come—time is the nervous eye of the rat in a jar

in the laboratory of the mad scientist who everyone

goes out of their way to avoid. Under the half-moons
of her red fingernails the horses finished their last rides

in the heat of the desert, which was her room. The stockings

of her youth were caught in the branches of the alder tree
outside her window. She was restless like a girl dressing

and undressing. I pushed my palm into the end of a pin

rather than hear her moaning. *What is it? What?* I asked
like a puppet with a string pulled backwards with a sting.

She was the one I couldn't unwrap. I was the musician

playing for her soul. But with souls you cannot bargain.

First Time

I was a virgin but I knew the messy sexual hunger of the word *ah*.

It was like two wires crossing that never should. It was like
    the invention
of sound for the deaf. Through my brother's great, slightly open,
    bedroom door

I saw two heads bobbing for apples on the pillow, their mouths in the
    shape of *ah*,

the wet crystals of each breath falling on their faces. I heard that final
    ah they made—
the room ripped apart, the wild, injured noise of a wounded dog.

Hello, little brother, my brother said. *I hope we weren't too loud*,
    the girl said.

I couldn't speak; the wind drifting through me as if through a cow's
    skull in the desert.
I watched their fingers sift through each other's hair again, pulling at
    the roots

of everything that had come before, and everything that would come after.

The girl had this way of murmuring, narrating in the dark. I pushed
    the door
further open. *Ah that's good*, she moaned. *Now you.*

My Twentieth Century

After I kissed Catherine I told her to call me Jay

because I wanted her to know my real name
because I wanted her to know who I really was.

She said to call her Catherine. I loved the way

she let me carry my secrets around and every now
and then, at noon or sunset, drop one on her foot.

See how heavy it is, I said, how the suffering goes on

after the suffering is over. I loved the way
she listened without listening when I couldn't change.

I loved the way she changed before the dark did,

the woman inside of her stepping out of her jeans.
I loved how she would curl up under the blanket

and get smaller like a shirt folding in on herself

until she was no larger than the size of her shoulder
leaning into mine. I loved how her breathing swelled

and came apart with the smell of lilacs from a garden

at the end of the street. I loved how her body shook
like a wild instrument with all this music inside it.

Saved

I want the body I grew up with

lying beside Beth Gold in the basement
of her father's house in Bellmore, Long Island.

By the fifth time she kissed me

I slipped off my shoes
and stared and stared at her face

until the need to be me disappeared.

Even when we were through touching,
leaning into each other,

my hand was still in a bandage

burned by my mother's cigarette,
its ashes descending in every cell.

And I pulled off the dressing

and showed her the scar
just to remind us of how lucky we were.

Middle Age

Many of my friends are alone
and know too much to be happy
though they still want to dive
to the bottom of the green ocean
and bring back a gold coin
in their hand. A woman I know wakes
in the late evening and talks
to her late husband,
the windows blank photographs.
On the porch, my brother,
hands in pockets,
stares at the flowing stream.
What's wrong? Nothing.
The cows stand
in their own slow afternoons.
The horses gather
wild rose hips in the sun
the way I longed for someone
long ago. What was it like?
The door opening
and no one on either side.

Something Beautiful

I was born in love
with the world

which I thought was made for me.

And when I was lucky
I was the hero

of a story.

It has been an odd reason
for urging on.

Here and there a distant oak
would interest me

as if material for the night's dream.

And then a poem, or prose, or something
impossible to read

and I had the power over its meaning.

Pigs

When I was a boy the one bad

creature I heard of was pigs,
pigs who rolled in the slime advocating

laziness, poor eating habits, the unimportance

of cleaning, staying in the deep mud
instead of walking a short distance to wash

in the pond. Lethargic, ragged-eared, pink-rusted,

droopy-tailed, heavy-loaded, dull-eyed pigs.
Pigs, who I learned later,

greet each other snout to snout

and at night snuggle up close to one another
and, for some unexplained reason,

sleep nose to nose; pigs who play with piglets

with immense patience, sniffing and nibbling
on them gently before pushing them aside

for another piglet.

Maybe I was absent the day in school
when the teacher said pigpens are often small

and dark, pigs nosing at straw to make a nest

for another litter taken away, adopted,
moved to an animal house, because

I thought pigs lived on farms with rolling hills

and green fields and cool winds
banging slowly against the barn doors.

Charles Darwin wrote: "the sooner the pig is fattened

for the butcher, the better." F. E. Zeuner, the historian, said
"unlike cattle, pigs cannot be driven

and their meat is prone to spoiling and so

we despise them." And William Youatt, the author
of the first book on pigs, published in 1847, wrote,

"pigs have feelings in common with each other

and in their eyes is a question for us, Why are you doing this to me?"
I thought I followed the pig

when my mother said that if I didn't clean my face

I would get pig's-eye,
or that my room was dirty as a pigsty,

or that I squinted in the sun like a pig

with small, black-beady eyes
but now I know I was trying like the pig

to get a better view of the world.

Now I know pigs dream and see colors,
pigs move a bale of straw with their snouts

so they can stand on the hay

and look out over the gate;
pigs have an ultrasensitive upward-whining groan

which seems to curve off the edge of their snouts

when in desire or distress—*oink, oink, oink, oink*—
to signal the other pigs to rush over,

which I once thought was a dirty and dumb sound.

The Birthday

I'm becoming more like my father: I rarely have sex.

What do I expect when the women I meet are always
my mother? Lately, I never go out anymore,

except once for minor surgery, and to see a live performance

of a woman smearing chocolate
on herself. I'd rather have surgery.

And I hate to admit it but I was uncomfortable

when my old girlfriend visited. No place to hide.
You never really try, she said. You just think you do.

If she really cared, she would know it was just the kind
of thinking I thought would make me a poet.

Just now, I am almost cheerful. It might be my friends talking.

Still, life is always going to be lonely. Why does this,
how can it possibly, still, be a surprise?

Fifty

Then there was the moment the flames assembled on top

of the blue birthday candles bringing their news of the luminous
wax toppling hissing of the passing of time

while I sat still, in the dark, as if inside a church,

asking for what I had asked for a thousand times,
my breath turned inside out in a sign of surrender.

How I Am

When I talk to my friends I pretend I am standing on the wing

of a flying plane. I cannot be trusted to tell them how I am.
Or if I am falling to earth weighing less

than a dozen roses. Sometimes I dream they have broken up

with their lovers and are carrying food to my house.
When I open the mailbox I hear their voices

like the long upward-winding curve of a train whistle

passing through the tall grasses and ferns
after the train has passed. I never get ahead of their shadows;

I embrace them in front of moving cars.

I keep them away from my misery
because to say I am miserable is to say I am like them.

Living

(after Stephen Dunn)

Just when it seemed my mother couldn't bear

one more needle, one more insane orange pill,
my sister, in silence, stood at the end

of the bed and slowly rubbed her feet,

which were scratchy with hard, yellow skin,
and dirt cramped beneath the broken nails,

which changed nothing in time except

the way my mother was lost in it for a while
as if with a kind of relief that doesn't relieve.

And then, with her eyes closed, my mother said

the one or two words the living have for gratefulness;
which is a kind of forgetting, with a sense

of what it means to be alive long enough

to love someone: *Thank you,* she said. As for me,
I didn't care how her voice suddenly seemed low

and kind, or what failures and triumphs

of the body and spirit brought her to that point—
just that it sounded like hope, stupid hope.

Eternity

A poem written three thousand years ago

about a man who walks among horses
grazing on a hill under the small stars

comes to life on a page in a book

and the woman reading the poem,
in the silence between the words,

in her kitchen, filled with a gold, metallic light,

finds the experience of living in that moment
so clearly described as to make her feel finally known

by someone—and every time the poem is read,

no matter her situation or her age,
this is more or less what happens.

Arrow Breaking Apart

While lovers sleep, I dig my nails into the earth,

holding up traffic. Just now a cloud has pulled up
while I was talking to the Emptiness

of the Universe and my voice plugged into the waves

at the bottom of the ocean.
My heart is taped up like a child's drawing

of the moon over the broken window of the sky

where the wind always comes back to fill my lungs.
I will dance on my shadow. I will open my mouth

with the air inside my mother's coffin.

I will be the arrow breaking apart in the body
of the blackbird, which appears at my window, singing.

Smoke

A woman is loosening the dark from me

with her mouth because I can't do it myself.
Now her breath is moving over me

the way wind drifts in a circle above water

and then goes on moving through the sky.
You OK? I can see the light leaking through

the small window before the sky will rush in

and feel the silence that carries the river along
in the deepest surf of the blood.

William Blake saw angels in his wife's hair.

I see shiny waves in a woman's hair like bits
of light tossed in the air and strewn with stars.

Is she the secret my body has kept from me?

Am I to be born again in the right flesh?
And then she throws her tongue like a match,

my body swelling and coming apart with the smell

of smoke as if a bullet were passing through it.

Summer Night

A man gets up from the chair in the restaurant and stands outside

on the sidewalk and strikes a match and holds the flame a little
ahead of the tip of a cigarette and breathes in, his head lifted,

inhaling the little puffs of smoke, and the scent of dark coffee

from a café at the end of the street, and even the warm white light
of the lampposts, and, sensing the pale humidity of time, he wants to stay,

quite unexpectedly, from now on, amidst the passing cars and people.

Travelers Anonymous

My name is Jason

and I've been in New York City
for six days now

but I wonder where else I could be—

maybe meeting the woman of all places

maybe reinventing the sunlight

or a telephone for the deaf.
Last night I walked to the blue car

hunched over on four wheels

at the end of the street,
and held myself down in the seat

while I gripped both hands

around the leather steering wheel.

Photograph

My mother so long ago, so young, so beautiful—it's not possible.
Surely she is still somewhere combing
away at her hair; that's why the air is so fragrant
and the sheets in disarray when I awaken.

part two

The Good Son

If God had come to me and said,
if you are willing to forget your self

you will find the cure for heart attacks and compose
the greatest symphonies,

I wouldn't have been sure of my answer.
Because there wouldn't have been enough

attention to my suffering. And that's unforgivable.
But I keep on forgiving myself

with God's love. And it's strange I should say this
because my mother died of a heart attack

after months in a hospital room full of a silence
that lodged itself like a stone in her throat.

And she thought I was wonderful

and would do anything for her.

The New Year

I will dive to the bottom of the hotel pool and find my mother's hairpin.

With the mouth of a drowning woman on my lap,
I will add her breath to mine. In the dark, I will lay the thin white sheet

of the moonlight over the blue plums of my wife's breasts.

With the new planet I discovered just when I thought I was losing
    my sight,
I will love another man because I will be a woman.

Everything important will never as yet have happened. Let it happen.

I will throw a lit match on the secrets my body
has kept from me and stand in the fire. The people I have sawed in half

will appear in my bedroom mirror, getting dressed.

The Story

One night, while my mother slept,

I read a story by Raymond Carver about a man
who kept finding his true love but always

got the address wrong. To look again was all he could do.
Once he offered to trade his shoes for a bus ticket

to ride past the great churches of wood and dust of Indiana.
And then he silently undressed himself in a room

at the end of a hall. Which is a place I know. Only
when I go there, love be damned. Get it myself, I say.

But that's wrong. I want to be lifted above the walls of my cell.
But I'm scared I can only be this body

that casts one shadow. It can't be the passing of years that kills
the man in the story. But it is. Just off the road.

Hospital

While the machine sucks the black suds

from my mother's blood and then sends it back
stinking clean into the pistol-tube nailed down

into her chest, I climb out of my shoes and slip

a cotton swab of water between her teeth,
her dentures sliding off the back porch

of her mouth. Nobody knows, nobody can ever know

how she has to pee, wrapped in a diaper.
But can't. The yellow eggs she ate one hour ago

already the shit in her bowels. And lonely,

head-hanging-from-the-balcony-of-her-body lonely,
darkest-passage-from-the-hairless-vagina lonely.

But brave. But lonely. Because I did not stay all night.

Because I won't. Because I'm going to pull out
the one bone that hurts her the most and break the back

of every word I ever said to her. The world is evil,

mother, and I am, too.

Finally, It Comes

Sometimes, late at night, I am the most burdened

like the blue plum in the bowl
left out all winter on the bedroom dresser.

Only man at midnight, I am like an emperor

whose robes have stopped flowing.
In bed I hang upside down like the body of a woman

inside the mouth of the lion.

Morning I cut my lips on a peach against my mouth.
I walk the coast of my life again. And still

I don't know where I am. Or who is beside me.

I stare at my weakness like a painter
staring at his last painting. All the ears of deer turn back

when I lean toward the river.

The Change

Your unmistakable breasts, plain, finely wrinkled, strained

but not crushed. You were no longer embarrassed to be naked
each time you undressed. And I didn't turn my gaze downward.

All your beautifulness, despite the loose skin hanging inches
from your bones. And the unshaven legs.

You weren't thinking you could rest against me either, even

when you tried. Thank you, mother. You let me see you unprotected,
full of doubt, miserable. So I could know you were still alive,

so I could know what loving someone looked like.

Provincetown

I bought a three hundred dollar black leather jacket

in Northern Lights to eliminate the cause of war
and my own intolerance. The lesbian saleswoman,

nose slightly pulled up by a gold ring, and beautiful breasts

rubbing up against her blouse, stood so close I inhaled
her breath. I left pizza crust on the bench beside Town Hall

promising to bless any creature who would swallow it.

Some sexual aroma hung from a slim-hipped
sweet-talking cross-dresser;

I was lonely again like the window of George's Pizzeria

when the sunlight passes through it.
So I burned a tattoo on my left arm of a snake wrapped in a snake

as a symbol of the power I don't have. I didn't.

I looked out the window at the ocean.
Time, I thought, which takes everything but itself, fuck you.

Poetry

What I am saying is not my true condition.

And what do I do if I am but am not?

I have my own life but it is not persuasive to me.

What she was doing, there was no way to remember it.

I can never find a color I love.

I believe I will love but get the day wrong.

I don't do what my friends say I do.

The Return

My only mother, who lost sixty pounds, tried to stand up

in the bathroom and fell backwards on the white linoleum floor
in the first hour of the morning and was carried to the bed

in the nurse's arms and then abruptly opened her eyes, later,

the room dark, and twisted the needles in her arms and talked
to her dead friend, Rosie, and heard the doorbell ring

as though in the kitchen in the old place deciding

if she should answer, and rubbed the circle on her finger

where the wedding ring once was while slipping downward
on the sheets like a body without limbs and I slid

my good arms beneath her armpits and pulled her bony

body up against the two thin pillows. And then,
when she was asleep again, I walked down the hallway's arc

of yellow light, ghosts hovering on either side of the doors

of rooms where the strange sickness of being alive
was the last thing between dreaming and eternity

which closes like the ocean closes over the blue-starry body

which does not stop, and I understood again
that we never come back, and upright, with everything

that takes its life seriously, I returned to my mother.

Daughter

I don't remember the face exactly, but the girl I saw once

in the upstairs window of a house in the middle of a town
in Vermont while I was driving one summer afternoon was exactly

like the face of the daughter I thought

I would have. Was she trying to tell me something? The scrape
of the tires against the road stopped me from listening

for a while. Sometimes I wake up, up to the shoulders in emptiness

but then I remember what I remember of the face of the girl.
Where is she now? And it marks my vanishing.

Jacksonville, Vermont

Because I am not married, I have the skin of an orange

that has spent its life in the dark. Inside the orange I am blind.
I cannot tell when a hand reaches in and breaks

the atoms of the blood. Sometimes a blackbird will bring the wind

into my hair. Or the yellow clouds falling on the cold floor
are animals fighting each other

out of their drifting misery. All the women I have known

have been ruined by fog and the deer crossing the field at night.

Hope

Hope is all the way down
in the self

from where it can never be judged

when we are more like children
than we want to be

waking up,

and choosing which stories
we will tell.

part three

Appointment

When I visit the doctor, I am reminded that I, too, was sick.

And still am. Not because of sadness or because in 1976
I wasn't kind to my father at his deli on Kings Highway,

Brooklyn. I swept the floor without talking to him, without

knowing what work was. And money. When I looked,
he was slumped in a chair, pulling the ends of his mustache.

I'm not sick because of anything; just because. The doctor

digs his fingers into the liquid tumors growing just beneath
the skin of my neck and in the crossword puzzle of hair

under my armpits; I imagine the yellow leaves hanging

from the branches of a willow tree that fall in Paris long ago.
A young Chinese nurse stands in the doctor's office, alone

in her body as if under a streetlamp, the white neon light

of her breath going out of her, going out. I slip my pants below
my knees. When I was in love I could not get used to the hours

with someone in them. What have you been feeling? Doctor asks.

Nothing. I turn away and cough, and, in that moment, when
the doctor is feeling my grainy-skinned quiet pair of balls

in that precise and careful way, I am ashamed that something

in me, some absence about myself, some loneliness I've never
understood, which sometimes disappoints, but which sometimes

shows me who I am, is made better by his slight touch.

Afterwards

I remember the shame I felt after the news

of the illness that I was not as lovable
as I thought. I must have done something

wrong. And then

I was content in my disappointment
which kept me alone. It was a kind of courage

that allowed me to go on without comfort.

It was a kind of beauty when there was no one
I wanted near.

Sickness

I am always better behaved

beside the man
with the big brown tumor

growing just below his chin—

wanting to be worth the horror
he lavishes,

wanting to be good enough

to join his suffering
with a little of my own.

I go out of my way to avoid

staring at him
but the staring

in silence,

is a kind of tenderness
because it is so blind.

He knows, doesn't he—
how much I need

his sickness,

and the God that made it—
how strengthened I am

by the cruelty of it.

Bone Marrow Transplant

Maybe this is the event I should take that girl to;

her eyes always watering as if she were an old city
like Venice, sinking under the weight of the past;

one more disappointment could break her.

At least then there would be moments of romance
when the marrow turns the color of the moon

and is gone. At least then the expectation of love

might rise over the gun-metal iron bed
like the faint odor of a foreign perfume.

Killing Frost

In that private hospital room,

which I paid for, I could not sleep,
because the bed was small

and its white sheets too thin

and matted with a sticky substance
that smelled of formaldehyde.

In the dark I could hear the nurses

make their animal calls.
I was hungry as if in the quiet

before a hunt
and stayed close to the orange chemical

passing through the rubber tube

and into the hole the needle made
in the right arm

without looking into it.

When I woke up in the morning
I was curled up under the blanket

like a wolf licking its paws

stained with the blood
from all of my good friends,

their hearts eaten out.

The Knot

I'm not sure how to make the knot just right—I was given

the orange and black tie, although it's old, impossibly skinny,
by Allen Ginsberg's assistant; he has to give away

hundreds of unfashionable, stringy ties from a box—

the white flowered, the bow tie, the rusty clip that hooks
one end to the other, even the red power ties—

before he can fulfill Allen's last wishes. *Throw away the yellow ones,*

Allen wrote. This is all happening on an afternoon in October, 1997,
six months after Allen died. It's a beautiful day in the century.

People slip into the office, their open shirts suddenly closed

with the cross of one end over the other.
Meanwhile, I go to the bathroom to fix the knot in the mirror—

lines from Allen's poem, "Sunflower Sutra," are on the wall,

*We're not our skin of grime, we're not our dread bleak dusty imageless
locomotive*—and I pause, shirt open, shoulders upright,

reading, rubbing the tie together.

Reverie

The pregnant teenager alone on the chair in the ward

and then the smell of leaves before the rain
and, after. I think for a while I'll go back

to that summer so long ago

but now the shifting wind is another person entering
the room and wearing a mask

with only the eyes exposed

and the sun is a gold watch setting in the white pocket
of the doctor.

Winter

If I could stop hoping for a month,

stop praying for a month, I could be alone again
with God in the old way, in a room at the end

of a hall and ask why it gets late early now.

Paris, 1980

I didn't know who I would be. Or where I was going.
Or how much money I would make.

Back then I wanted to be unknown. But beautiful.

Like some bird. At least. I was living with a woman
who stepped out of the back of the portable radio,

secret and hidden, singing. I had the money, modest and golden,

my father gave me. So I would not have to beg.
I wish I had had a vision strolling along the Seine.

I wish I would have given the man what he wanted

when he awoke me from sleeping on a park bench.
What was my life to me then?

Life After We Know It

Irene, I am passing a brush through my hair
and buttoning the buttons of my best shirt.

Everything is almost ready
but nothing is happening for certain.

Like the day after you left,
when I kept thinking you might leave.

As if you weren't around anymore
to ask about my life.

This is the story so far: getting ready, making plans,
getting ready.

Like today, when I hurried down the middle
of the street,

I was standing still.
I am a childless man. I should have loved you.

October

The cold foreheads of apples graze the ground

with nothing on but their torn green jackets.
When I step into the shower

I am like the president of the United States

stepping up to the microphone,
and everyone in the world is waiting

to hear if I will be lying again.

Who rearranged the blue sheets on the bed?
Who stretched the calendar?

Who pulled the shades down in the afternoon?

It's like I am wearing the white sleeves
of the doctor who cannot check the samples

of his own breath. I should push myself

into the pants of a new profession.
I should stand up with my fears like the butcher

waking up in the belly of the cow.

Company

I've been avoiding my illness
because I'm afraid

I will die and when I do,
I'll end up alone again.

If You Want to Know

What face would the nurse want to be staring at more than mine—
    bluest eyes,
ivory skin,

full lips, scruffy beard, black hair falling forward on the forehead?
I am tired of looking good to get her attention, but I like the way it
    makes her stop

and think about how beautiful I am, and more beautiful with all
    that is going
on inside

me. Cancerous cells speeding past the off-ramps of the highways
    to gather
in the lymph nodes and then attack the lungs, liver and spleen—

while outside the nurse watches the beauty of my face go on and on.

Coda

And now I know what most deeply connects us after that summer so
    many years ago,

and it isn't poetry, although it is poetry, and it isn't illness, although we
    have that in common,
and it isn't gratitude for every moment, even the terrifying ones, even
    the physical pain,

though we are grateful, and it isn't death, though we are halfway through

it, or even the way you describe the magnificence of being alive, with
    your long blowing hair
and reflection in the windowpane of the video store, though it is beauti-
    ful, it is; but it is

that you're my friend out here on the far reaches of what humans can
    find out about each other.

The Source

I close my eyes and try to remember when I hardly

knew anything, anyone, without memory, without knowing it.
I close my eyes and try to remember when I hardly

said anything to anyone, without language,

without thinking again about what I thought.
I close my eyes and groan to remember when it was dark

the way the homeless groan to forget it is.

Before the great jaw, before the heart clasped tight,
barely moving, before the breath-burst,

before the actual blood, before I lied, before I was afraid;

I close my eyes and try to remember the first purple
of the first iris of the first spring,

when I was unopposed, when I started to die,

buoyant, fragrant, shuddering with love.

part four

The Party

And that's how it is; everyone standing up from the big silence

of the table with their glasses of certainty and plates of forgiveness
and walking into the purple kitchen; everyone leaning away from the
    gas stove

Marie blows on at the very edge of the breaking blue-orange-lunging-

forward flames to warm another pot of coffee, while the dishes pile up
    in the sink,
perfect as a pyramid. *Aaah,* says Donna, closing her eyes,

and leaning on Nick's shoulders as he drives the soft blade of a knife

through the glittering dark of the leftover chocolate birthday cake.
That's it; that's how it is; everyone standing around as if just out of
    the pool,

drying off, standing around, that's it, standing, talking,

shuffling back and forth on the deck of the present
before the boat slowly pulls away into the future. Because it hurts

to say goodbye, to pull your body out of the warm water;

to step out of the pocket of safety, clinging to what you knew,
or what you thought you knew about yourself and others.

That's how it is, that's it, throwing your jacket over your shoulders

like a towel and saying goodbye Victoria goodbye Sophie goodbye
Lili goodbye sweetie take care be well hang in there see you soon.

Upon Hearing the Experimental Drug Did Not Work

When I stared at the squirrel,

in the last light of day, for a long time
I must have looked away—
its curved cheeks were like the sides of boats
its dark eyes seemed loose and shiny
as if from weeping—
the small nose. I looked again—
remembering how important everything once was,
ready for my shoulders to blast apart
to make room for a new life
at the touch of someone's hand—
and the creature was lost, hiding in secret,
in the green and yellow grass.

Tuttle Crossing, Ohio

Sometimes I bring my illness to the field,

where the trees stand
like the conductors of the dark.

Digging into a pocket of the earth,

I am always grateful to find a note
from my mother

just as the wind pulls up

with the upward whining of an ambulance;
One more year. One more year.

Heal yourself, the owl says.

In the grasses and ferns,
the crickets ring like cowbells

and the bright orange threads of stars

come off in my hands.
I lie down without sleep like a hunter

below the ceiling of his cave

where there are drawings of animals
without arms and legs.

Fall

When I look at the wind
          in the trees
all I see are trees
          moving in their way.

If I want to see the wind,
          I have to see my rage—

What has gone wrong, I ask.

There, inside the branches,
          is the one thing I don't have, stirring,

as if it were a beauty not (never)
to be had just yet.

This is a letter, you could say,
          about how much I need from you.

    I was led into these thoughts
by the beauty of the morning,
    the light lying down in the low grasses.

When I sat down
    every year of my life was right there—

like a link to childhood,
    those beginnings we hold sacred

in the absence of God.

Looking for Ohio

I.

I am walking in the supermarket at night

where the heart is a tough customer trying to survive.
I am touching the round blossom of a peach

but feel the cold roadside stone-pit of its price.

I don't need my eyes until I see the lopsided chin
of the teenager cursing the cantaloupes;

or the small black holes the needles of perishing

make in the veins of the old woman;
her throat bent back like a small bird.

I have to learn more about kindness from her.

I have to grind down the lead of my disappointment
into a smaller and smaller complaint

among the speechless shifting shapes walking

through aisle after aisle of every harm and grace
that has come before them and everything

that will come after—

in the marriage of knowing we have and knowing
we will never have enough. Muzak to memory

and memory traveling note after note to the past,

with its charity of lies and prison-scribbling of light;
I have to turn the endless maze of loss to humility

and a name in the heaven of housewares intersection,

where the loneliest one with no face keeps appearing
and whispering sweetly into my human ear,

if you ever want to know me, now.

II.

Like every white horse sitting on the other side

of the fence in the slow hours
of the afternoon. I know to move is to be still;

like the apple on the table

turning by degrees into a perfect sphere
always on the perimeter of taste, touching the stem,

the naked woman. This is the first meditation;

the shoes carefully arranged on the blue carpet
in the closet, the ill-fitting jacket, a limp thing

hanging on a hook, heavy with longing,

the shirt unbuttoned. I'm still here from there before;
a taxicab stub, the snowy corner of a building,

Sophie Marie Lucie Tony, a window going dark,

the trees still dressed up and ready to turn
toward each other and swing when the wind starts;

and later the lion in me clearing his throat

making love in the presence of my shadow.

III.

Over the black socks lifted from the black rug,

over the loose wires of water at the long faucet's edge,
over the glowing tip of the single cigarette

curling off the reddish end of my mother's

twenty-two-year-old lips,
over the crumpled sheets, over the narrow bed,

I sit in the middle of illumination

I see the white downpour of the white hair
of my mother's face,

as though she can't believe I have come,

or is trying to remember me,
with her small hands too small for holding—

and my legs, bound together, coming down

again from the body. Maybe we don't die, exactly;
but turn over into silence.

Or else there is no such thing as the spirit.

Or else I am the exits of the maze I have blocked,
admiring the walls of isolation, the dead ends.

IV.

I am walking in the shopping malls at night

where the heart is a tough customer
trying to survive,

and the loneliest one who traveled light years

appears as if on an orbiting dance floor—
with the music of everything that has come before

and the music of everything that will come after playing

every day will be the last day of the last day
when the windows are opened and the good winds

circling the great globe are blowing up the last moments

when you know you will never know enough.

Afterbody

After the chemo and the throwing up,

after the passion of a life upset,
after I watched the color of the skin turn yellow—

my thoughts more and more about things

that never happened—after I spent many nights
alone, happy for the police dramas on television,

I kept to myself.

The cancer saved me from having to go
to another book party

from having to ask M. to come back

who, after all, had fallen out of love
because I was different now, thin,

bone and severity, free to consider

my absence, where nothing aches
and the messy sexual hungers are far off

in the past. After I slept for days,

after the dazzle of wild, repeatable dreams,
there was no afterlife,

just the same way from the bed

to the bathroom and back again
without the body.

Ocean

Goodbye again. Say there is a little song in my head

and because of it I can't sleep or change my mind
about the future. Now the song runs all the way down

to the beach where I sit as if the sky

were my room now. No one, not even you,
can hear me singing. Not even me.

As if the music rose from the mouth of the ocean.

No mouth. Like rain before it reaches us.
Like wind twirling dresses on the clothesline.

Who has no one has the history of the ocean.

Lord, give me two more days. So that
the last moments may be with someone.

Between

To feel the elegance there one more time

the lavish nakedness left over from kissing
the secret hairs hanging with wetness

is to put one finger, and then another finger,

slowly into her
as if into the body of another animal,

as if into a well of dreaming.

At Sunset

Your death must be loved this much.

You have to know the grief—now.
Standing by the water's edge,

looking down at the wave

touching you. You have to lie,
stiff, arms folded, on a heap of earth

and see how far the darkness

will take you. I mean it, this, now—
before the ghost the cold leaves

in your breath, rises;

before the toes are put together
inside the shoes. There it is—the goddamn

orange-going-into-rose descending

circle of beauty and time.
You have nothing to be sad about.

Alone for the Fifth Day

When I look at the ocean for a long time, the blue

and restless driven waves, I keep looking, I keep looking,
I keep looking at the waves swaying in the wind

like a metronome, wired for the sound of a sleeping heart,

and I keep looking with the silence of the sun
on the windowpane, and I keep looking and do not stop

looking deeper into waves as if into the middle

of a woman's body, where the soul and spirit
have no human bonds, and I begin never to turn away

from looking though I am frightened but keep looking

beyond what I know until I can hardly think or breathe
because I have arrived, with the need to be me disappearing

into the beautiful waves, reflecting no one, nothing, no one.

Not Sleeping

It's dark for a reason. So just lie down.

Maybe you inhabit a death.
Maybe no-love. Or worse, love.

Maybe nothing but the loose end

of your voice unable to reach you.
It feels like. Don't think about that.

A whiteness, less white suddenly.

Untitled

If there is no cure, I still want to correct a few things

and think mostly of people, and have them all alive.
I want a door opening in me that I can enter

and feel the clarity of evening and the stars beginning.

One after another, I want my mistakes returning
and to approach them on a beach like a man

for whom there is no division between one way or another.

My most faithful body, you are not in the best of shape,
far from the glitter of the river in which you once swam.

But I want good tears when I stand on the street

and, from the sky, drifts down the finest mist on my face.
Not everything is given and it should not permit sadness.

Let me
Let me keep on describing things to be sure they happened.

Afterword

Jason Shinder left instructions that the four of us serve as his literary executors after his death. Our first and most important job was to edit the book he'd been writing. As close friends of Jason's, each of us had seen many versions of these poems. Each of us knew how obsessively he reworked poems, and how he had constantly reordered the manuscript. With so many versions of individual poems and so many versions of the manuscript, how were we to compose the book he had in mind? We couldn't know, exactly.

Jason must have smiled imagining his four dear and very different friends trying to come to poetic consensus. Working alone and together—in person, on telephones, through emails, reading poems aloud, ordering and reordering pages—we slowly came into confidence that this collection is close to what Jason would have wanted.

Sophie Cabot Black
Lucie Brock-Broido
Tony Hoagland
Marie Howe

Acknowledgments

Thanks to the editors of the following magazines and journals in which some of the poems in this collection, sometimes in different versions, first appeared: *American Poetry Review, Five Points, Laurel Review, Ploughshares, Provincetown Arts, Slate,* and the *Writer's Chronicle.*

The following poems, sometimes in different versions, also appeared in the chapbook *Arrow Breaking Apart* published by Arrowsmith Press in 2006: "The Pitch of Childhood," "How I Am," "October," "My Twentieth Century," "Hospital," "Eternity," "Daughter," "The Alder Tree," "The Return," "Bone Marrow Transplant," "Jacksonville, Vermont," "The Change," "Appointment," "The Party," "At Sunset," "Summer Night," "Finally, It Comes," "The New Year," "Tuttle Crossing, Ohio," "Provincetown," and "Arrow Breaking Apart."

The poem "Living" first appeared in the *New Yorker.* It also appeared in the anthology *Best American Spiritual Writing 2009* (Mariner Books, 2008).

The poem "Eternity" also appears in the anthology *By Heart: Poetry as a Doorway to the Soul* (Hay House, 2009).

The poems "The Change" and "The New Year" also appeared in the anthology *Never Before: Poems About First Experiences* (Four Way Books, 2005).

Jason Shinder is the author of three collections of poetry, *Every Room We Ever Slept In, Among Women,* and *Stupid Hope,* and a chapbook of poems, *Arrow Breaking Apart.* He edited numerous anthologies, including *The Poem That Changed America: "Howl" Fifty Years Later,* and served as series editor of the annual *Best American Movie Writing.* He received awards and fellowships from the Fine Arts Work Center in Provincetown, Massachusetts, the California State Arts Council, the National Endowment for the Arts, and the Yaddo Corporation, among others. Shinder was on the faculty of the graduate writing programs at Bennington College and the New School. He founded and served as director of the YMCA National Writer's Voice and YMCA of the USA Arts and Humanities, and he also directed the Sundance Institute's Writing Program. He was born in Brooklyn, New York, in 1955 and split his time between New York City and Provincetown, Massachusetts, until his death in 2008.

CPSIA information can be obtained
at www.ICGtesting.com
Printed in the USA
LVHW082357290822
727156LV00015B/1152